this is
MADNESS

HAT JUGGLING 101 FOR SUCCESSFUL SALES LEADERS

JOE KLEHA

This is Madness: Hat Juggling 101 For Successful Sales Leaders

© 2023 Joe Kleha

ISBN 979-8-9875738-0-8 (paperback)
ISBN 979-8-9875738-1-5 (eBook)

Cover design, editing & layout by megs Thompson – megswrites llc

www.inomniaparatuspublishing.com

For those who live and thrive in this madness.

TABLE OF CONTENTS

This is Madness

My name is Joe, and I'm a sales leader. It may seem like a silly way to introduce myself, but this profession is quite addicting. We learn to look past the long hours, exhausting travel, frustrating days, weeks, and months. We can't remember the slump of 2015, because the next year we went to Mexico for a Sales Excellence award trip. We are sales leaders, and we choose to be the tip of the revenue spear. As such, we embrace the ups and downs, focusing on delivering the numbers necessary.

When I first started writing this book, I didn't really have a "plan." In truth, I wanted to help my business grow and hopefully pass on some of the hard learned lessons from my years spent managing people. I felt like I had so many little tools and tricks, that there had to be at least a nugget, or two that other sales leaders could pull from these pages and implement within their own teams. Sure, there are a million books out there that bill themselves as the panacea for all your business-related issues, but that's not the purpose of this book. I'm comfortable with being a single soul in the crowded field of business books, mainly because I genuinely believe that we stumble on the right book, the right message, the right lesson at the right time. By taking years to get to this point, I've expanded my own experience tenfold and candidly, allowed myself the opportunity to test and retest, the theories I'm sharing here.

Every subject covered within these pages has been tried and tested in real life. They're honest and effective techniques that'll help you build a better culture and develop your own high performing teams. It's my sincerest hope and desire that you, the reader, will be able to improve efficiency and increase productivity in a positive way.

Because I've been where you are, and I understand that time is one of the most precious resources you have, I've intentionally kept this book short. The last thing any of us want to do is pick up an unabridged version of the Bible, that instead of being read is just going to gather dust on a shelf. This book has been written to fit into your laptop bag and referenced as needed. Think "small but mighty." I've included a handful of pages at the end of the book, for taking notes, gathering thoughts, and passing your own learned experiences onto the next generation of successful sales leaders.

Being a sales leader is not an easy gig. Rest assured, I understand how strange and lonely this profession can be at times. But I'm also familiar with the incredible sense of satisfaction and fulfillment that comes with having coached and developed your people, your team, helping them to achieve their own successes beyond what they'd imagined possible.

Choosing to be a sales leader is absolute madness, and for those of us to choose the role, we wouldn't have it any other way. We crave the challenge and chase the fortune. I'm honored and humbled that you've chosen to add my book to your toolbox. I hope you enjoy.

Motivation

Motivation is kind of like Bigfoot. Most people would really like to believe he exists but can't prove it. They don't know where he comes from, how to find him, or why he's always hiding. Some people go so far as to spend their careers trying to prove his existence and are generally regarded as being two fries short of a happy meal. Where did we lose our faith? How do we get back to the wonder and open-mindedness that's required to be successful in business and life, and to believe in Bigfoot again?

Many years ago, I was coached that as a sales leader, I could not motivate anyone. At first, I was annoyed. Who was this guy? What did he know? Did he actually have any experience managing a team of salespeople? I sat there in the crowd initially stunned, and then my annoyance turned into a determination to prove that coach wrong. What an ignorant idiot, I thought. Silently in the room, I could tell that others were on my same wavelength. We had been required to attend this training, and this guy had just told us that everything we knew was a lie. And this was only day 1 of a three-day training in New Jersey. There was no way I was going to get through the next few days. No chance.

I'm pretty sure that my body language and facial expressions belied my lack of engagement. It's amazing, how time can slow to a crawl when we're uncomfortable and part of a captive audience. I stuck it out (mostly because I had no choice) and to be honest, it was one of the best trainings I ever attended. Part of me wonders if this is when the seed was planted for me to write this book, more than 10 years after the fact. We may never know.

Within a few hours my perspective started to shift. Slowly at first, but gaining momentum with every moment. The premise of that particular coach was simple: a salesperson either shows up with the motivation, or they don't. You can't buy it, teach it, or earn it. That was an ostensibly binary outlook. It begged the question; how do salespeople find success? How do they become top producers, top performers, elite sellers? Certainly, their sales leaders have something to do with it. Candidly, as a manager, you have very little to do with motivation. Cue the sad tubas.

Before you turn in your badge, rip up your coaching certifications, and slink away in defeat, stick with me for just a moment more. Sales leaders have two very big jobs as it relates to the motivation of their teams. In fact, one could say that those who understand, execute, and teach others this process are sorely underpaid.

So, what are the two functions of a true sales leader?

1. To recognize intrinsic motivation and visualize future potential.
2. To create an environment and culture that draws in high performers and allows them to reach their full potential.

If you think either of these two purposes is simple, think again. One requires keen and optimistic insight, and the other takes a lot of consistent hard work. Breaking each one down further, we can explore how to implement them in your specific organization.

Recognizing intrinsic motivation and visualizing future potential is a topic that will probably get you the most pushback. It takes a lot of time and effort, and your sales teams (specifically your front-line managers) will not get it right all the time. But, through trial and error, you can start to positively influence your teams, and by default, improve the culture in way that is magnetic and scalable. I separated these two point on purpose, because it is really challenging to see them as not being mutually exclusive. So, you may be wondering, how does one recognize intrinsic motivation and what does it look like? This is going to vary wildly from person to person. But, in the immortal words of Stephen Covey, *begin with the end in mind*. Lock yourself in a room. Then list out all the characteristics of your ideal top performer. Don't hold back here, put everything on paper. Maybe even break out the whiteboard to add or erase quickly. It's important that you do not list out emotions, but only facts. For example, instead of including "always smiling" write down "possesses a positive outlook." Once you have everything conceivable written out, walk away from it for the rest of the day. After letting your list sit for 24 hours, read through it again and add anything else you come up with. Take nothing off the list, unless it falls under feelings, emotions, or otherwise strays from fact. Then walk away again. By putting your list aside, you'll be able to come back to it with a fresh perspective. With better ideas, and a clear head.

Once you've reached the third day of your list making exercise, you're ready to put it to paper. Next to each listed characteristic, define it. What does "prompt" mean and look like? Odds are that your list will include the term "motivated," but you won't be able to define it quite yet. Leave that space blank and continue down your list, adding definitions and building out descriptions. Now, for the challenging part.

Take this list of characteristics and definitions, and create questions that help determine, based on their responses, whether the candidate you are interviewing, the employee you are coaching, or the peer you are interacting with possesses these skills and traits. Again, this is not and should not be easy. You're attempting to create a framework in your mind so that not only do you ask the right questions, but you'll also know when you find the right person or people, coach effectively to hone their skills, or puzzle through a strategy with a peer.

The underlying idea of this exercise is to not only understand the roles and what the perfect candidate looks like, but also to be able to communicate the qualities and to be able to communicate your ideas and vision both internally and externally. The result is twofold- a profile of a high performer, and the exact questions that should be asked during interviews, conversations, coaching's, etc. In the case of interviewing, you may choose to implement some sort of scoring system, though that is entirely up to you. Personally, I like assigning points to the questions written, because it keeps the process very objective and as you have interactions with more and more candidates, their answers and traits may begin to run together in your mind. Having a points system allows you to recall the content of each interview quickly and with much less confusion.

I feel it necessary to include a note here about how important it is to confirm that the questions you've drafted and intend to ask, are appropriate. I've seen many a well-intentioned manager get themselves into dicey situations because they didn't have someone else vet their questions prior to an interview. People management and all things HR will probably be the subject of another book. If your company is small and you don't have in-house HR support, now would be a good time to find a consultant you can partner with for interview guides as well as handbooks and policy templates. The main thing you want to avoid is changing questions between candidates. You'll never be able to compare performance in the interview if you're asking each candidate a different set of questions. When you visit a new city and ask about a good restaurant, the first clarifying question you will most likely get is about what type of cuisine or dining experience you'd like to have. It's not all that dissimilar to creating interview questions and processes.

The second part, after creating the framework, is being able to take the responses and actions you receive, and decide if this person will be able to consistently perform at a level that is higher than their peers. This takes a lot of practice and the ability to recall comparative performance in the interview and potentially on the job. A good way of finding a baseline is to look at your most respected top performer. Not just the one who always seems to crush their quota, but one who finds success almost as a byproduct of helping and mentoring others. These salespeople are often not at the very top, but consistently deliver strong results, usually in the face of significant headwinds. They may have lost a big client through no fault of their own, or when territory lines are redrawn. They will without hesitation raise their hand to volunteer for pilot programs, because they see the bigger picture. These salespeople are the ones who have characteristics that you want to replicate with new hires, creating not only the right environment where they can be successful, but also the culture that you want to foster within your organization.

The environment and culture must be guarded at all costs, because it is extremely hard to rebuild once lost. By allowing the right people to demonstrate the behaviors necessary for a sales culture to not only exist, but thrive, you're able to set the tone and clear expectations. Other, similar individuals will no doubt gravitate to this environment, thus creating a self-driven pattern of growth and development. It's worth noting that these salespeople are not always the norm. In fact, they often exhibit behaviors that run contrary to what most people think of when they consider top performers. Do not overlook a strong producer who is quiet because you think that you need a verbose cheerleader on your team. Your objective is to create a rising tide via your team, not to reinvent the wheel.

More importantly, through this entire process, you haven't attempted to motivate anyone. Instead, you've created the framework, the map of sorts, that attracts and supports the best fitting individuals for the job. When this comes together, it's quite a magical experience. Now, it should go without saying that even though you have an environment and culture of high performance, you will also have challenges and conflicts of personalities. That is inevitable. Coaching in those moments can look quite different because you're working on unique situations with individual, strong-willed people. However, it should not run counter to or compete with the non-negotiable culture of success that has been developed.

One of the easiest ways to begin the process of leveling up your team is to stack rank them. Include in the ranking the main attributes or behaviors that solidify their placement. For example, if one of your sales reps consistently has an enormous pipeline, that's a good foundational component of the job. Someone who always exceeds quota may be higher in the ranking but could stand to learn a lot from their peer. Perhaps instead of beating quota by 5%, if they increased their pipeline, they could plausibly beat quota by 25%.

Start thinking about how the attributes and behaviors are interrelated in the sales process for your team. When you set aside time for strategy (which you absolutely must do on a consistent basis), you should envision your team(s) as a biosphere of sorts. Everything works in symbiosis with everything else. Spending time drumming up leads is like planting seeds. Maintaining contact with the lead is watering. Opportunities are put into your pipeline as the plant begins to sprout. Like real life, a good harvest is not guaranteed, but there are things you can do to help affect the outcome.

By pairing tasks to the salesperson with the skill you need for that, you help leverage their strengths. Working on their areas of opportunity will come with time. It's important to help them see wins before you start challenging them to improve in a particular area. Remember that when you work with and coach your people, use "we" terms and not "I" or "you" words. Your job is to work together with your teams, not push with your title. True leaders do not need a position or nameplate with a fancy title to get results.

Newly promoted or hired sales leaders tend to attempt to bend the world to their will without having the experience of failure to temper their style. Yes, Patton did say that "A good plan violently executed now is better than a perfect plan executed next week", but that is only effective AFTER you have proven yourself and won the respect and loyalty of your team. Otherwise, you are the giant bull in the china shop and you will be viewed as reckless, not passionate. By consistently pairing tasks to the people and their skills, you will understand what certain employees are strong at, and where they have opportunities that need to be developed. Pushing too hard too soon only causes anxiety and stress. Unless dealing with a tenured rep, this will be a recipe for increased turnover, and most likely not success.

Pairing tasks to people also does something really special, it gives you an opportunity to not only show the employee that you are genuinely trying to develop them, but also allows you to gain insight into how they work. One situation that comes to mind for me occurred just a few weeks into a new role. We had an all-company meeting, and the CEO was hammering home a point about how people shouldn't waste time. Nothing new there. Later in the day, a very young employee was talking to me and showed me a funny video from *The Office* that related to an interaction we had previously. As I was speaking to and laughing with the other person, I was called out by the CEO and my SVP about how my actions ran counter to the message we had received a few hours before. In their eyes, neither of us was working. However, attempting to create robots or carbon copies of senior leaders runs completely undermines your ability to create an environment where people can be successful. Emotional intelligence goes a long way. In hindsight, I should have taken the moment to professionally coach up, and help them see things from my perspective, but instead I took my scolding and went back to my office. Not even a month into my role, and I knew it wouldn't last. Culture is and must be omnipresent in an organization, regardless of your level or title.

Pro tip: If you see your front-line managers in their office more than interacting with their employees (both work and non-work related), take away their chair. Building rapport and interpersonal relationships is one of the main skillsets of a strong leader. After a remodel in my building years ago, all the offices had glass walls in the front with a glass door. These doors by default closed unless propped open. So, I got a doorstop for my door. Actions will always speak louder than words.

Accountability

Accountability. Just saying the word out loud gives some individuals the perception of authority, while others cringe at the very sound. We've become conditioned to believe that accountability is a negative, punitive process. That everything we've done is apparently wrong because, well, someone needs to be held accountable. I have no idea where we went so wrong. It never used to be that way. Being held accountable meant that you were where the buck stopped. Sure, it's also the flip side of recognition, so accountability can be somewhat negative at times. It is, however, absolutely critical in order to have a high performing sales culture. Leaders take responsibility, not pass blame. They realize that if they are truly leading, then the direction, project, process, and eventual outcome are all tied to them, the leader. Good or bad, the leader is in charge.

So, how does this relate to salespeople? It's pretty much the same concept; if a salesperson sets a goal and does not achieve it, they should be held accountable. The opposite also holds true, if they set a goal and achieve it, they should be recognized. Where most leaders and managers get it wrong is in the consequences or rewards associated with these outcomes. Hitting quota for one month should probably not result in the award of a million-dollar bonus, nor should missing quota result in the loss of a hand. Both are extreme, but I think you get the point. Far too often managers and leaders over deliver on rewards or consequences, devastating the team culture. By doing so, employees view the culture as a pendulum or tennis match and get dizzy watching their poor leaders, and colleagues, bounce back and forth between extremes. If your team is always "afraid of what the boss will think," you have a massive culture problem on your hands. The only way to exorcise that issue is to start by looking in the mirror. We'll cover the introspection needed in a later chapter.

The correct and best way to coach salespeople is to follow the same repeatable patterns until it becomes muscle memory.

1. Define the goal for the month, quarter, year in a way that allows full and transparent understanding of what the end game truly is.
2. Build a strategy around the goal.
3. Develop executable tactics to achieve the goal via the strategy.
4. Review progress daily, weekly, and monthly. This may seem like overkill, but if something is off, you want to fix it quickly. Conversely, if things are going well, you want to replicate it.

Think of the above in terms of real life. Your "goal" is your end destination. In this example, let's say you are going to Cabo San

Lucas for a well-deserved vacation. That is your goal. It is the end point and purpose of your travels. Your strategy will probably be to fly or to drive from your current location, depending on where you live. The tactics are pretty obvious; book the hotel, buy a ticket or get your vehicle ready. Pack your clothes. And then start the journey. If you decided to drive, you will most likely be checking the map or GPS to confirm you're not headed to Detroit by mistake.

The crazy part is the above sounds like a no brainer, but when it comes to business and selling, people suddenly overcomplicate the heck out of it instead of maintaining a consistent, repeatable process.

Here's the reality, once you've created your environment and culture, and added in this process, it very quickly becomes your team's standard operating procedure. Without it, they will call you out. Those who don't are trying to hide. By combining culture and standards, you won't have any trouble identifying your team's underperformers. This is where accountability comes into play and the consequences should be tempered with caution. Just because a salesperson is underperforming, it does not mean that they have failed or need to be fired. In fact, the opposite approach should be attempted first. Coach and mentor. You will be able to quickly determine if it is skill or will. We'll cover that a bit later but keep it in mind as you work with your teams.

If you have a team member that's underperforming, the key is to address it quickly and head on. But don't rush to drop the hammer of justice on a salesperson who was having an off day. Instead, employing a bit of empathy (see chapter on Conflict), you can get to the root of the problem by allowing the salesperson to self-discover. This is much more powerful and positive then anything you could come up with. Your job as a sales leader or manager is to ask questions, to help others understand themselves, and when you do both of these, you'll continue to drive performance without having to be an ass.

"Despise not the day of small beginnings." That may or may not have been spoken by an angel, but it is most certainly true in business as well as life. The blue whale is the largest living animal, growing to almost 100 feet long and weighing nearly 200 tons! All that comes from a single cell. That cell splits and those cells split, and so on. The great Redwood trees have been documented to grow to over 300 feet tall yet begin as a seed. Even if that seed were the size of a sedan, it would still be impressive. Developing people and your teams really aren't all that different. It starts with an idea, or the thought of a strategy. Through patience and discipline, you can transform that ragtag bunch of newbies into world-class elite sellers.

Most younger sales leaders will make mistakes when it comes to holding people accountable, especially in the early part of their careers. I was absolutely one of those managers. Holding salespeople accountable is not done via title. It's done via partnership. Sales managers who manage through fear, will find that their teams are some of the least innovative. No one is willing to take even the smallest risk if they fear extreme consequences. Some of the best advice I was given helped me to create a safer environment for my team to make their own decisions. My Director told me once, "I'll never fault you for making what you thought was the best decision with the information you had. We can fix just about anything, and you will learn from your mistakes." Talk about liberating and opening the floodgates of innovation. It was like I finally received permission to push the boundaries, and my team responded beautifully.

Understanding your organization's sales process is critical. You as the leader must know it inside and out in order to be able to communicate it effectively with your teams. Let's look at a generic sales cycle as an example on how to hold salespeople accountable.

LEADS
+
OPPORTUNITIES
+
WINS
=
QUOTA ATTAINMENT

If you look at this and review it daily, weekly, and monthly, it becomes set in stone and you can easily coach to it, not beat up the salesperson. Your conversation should sound something like this:

"Congratulations on a fantastic month! You crushed quota at 111% to goal! How did you do that? I mean, you almost made it look easy. When we dig in a bit to the numbers, it looks like last month you had $150,000 in your pipeline, and this month you have $320,000. How do we replicate that? Is there anything you can think of that you're doing differently?"

Your individual and unique organization will determine if you work with leads or use specific naming conventions, but virtually every sales team uses some variation of this. So, if you do not use quota but instead use revenue targets, then that's ok. What terms are used becomes less relevant than following the formula that suits your company.

Notice the process and language, and how the leader starts by recognizing the work, gets granular, and then seeks to foster a partnership to recreate the success. Yes, it can be much simpler if the sales rep has a good month. So, what if they didn't hit quota and you need to hold them accountable? First, don't blow smoke. Reps can smell it, they expect it. Be direct, but provided that this individual isn't doing anything wrong, be sure to maintain empathy or you'll lose the battle, and you could irreversibly ruin your relationship with the person.

In the case of a bad month, it should sound more like this: *"Before we dig into last month, I wanted to see how you were doing. It was a tough month across the board, and out of the norm for you. What changed last month? I have my thoughts, but first, I'm sure you've done quite a bit of digging in yourself. Between the two of us, we can figure this out and get back on track this month. Sound good?"*

In order to hold someone accountable, you need to first ensure that they feel safe. Accountability isn't about assigning blame; it's making sure that top performers are held to a standard of excellence. Trust me, any strong salesperson beats themselves up more than enough, they don't need their manager or leader piling on. What they need, what they search for, is a leader who understands that sometimes things just don't go to plan. In those moments, they need a hand up, not a verbal bashing. And for the love of all that's holy, don't threaten them with discipline. If you're moving directly into putting them on a disciplinary plan after the first month of poor performance, you had better be prepared to sit in their seat for the next few months while you search for their replacement. If the direction is coming down from your boss, then you have failed leadership on your hands. That's a completely different problem that I will not address here. My point is that coaching needs to be an ongoing, daily, even hourly exercise. It shouldn't happen just because the month is over, or you're getting pressure from above you. If that's the case, you've failed as a leader and your culture will suffer until you can right the ship. Coaching as a punitive event or to check a box means that <u>you</u> need to be held accountable and <u>you</u> are the one who has lost your way.

Here's what most leaders fail to realize; accountability is something that top performers crave. Yes, they desire being held accountable, even if they do not come right out and say it. How many times have you heard your team ask where everyone else is? They want to see where they stack in relation to their peers. They need it like a fish needs water. Allowing transparency helps give them something to shoot for and something to chase.

Pro tip: if your sales teams are always preoccupied with chasing results or revenue, they most likely won't have time for inter-office drama. You're welcome.

Accountability creates boundaries and sets the expectations for the team and the individual. Without it, you may as well be in the wild West. Accountability puts the bumpers in the bowling lane. It's the lane markers on the highway. However you define it, stick with it. There is strategy in continuity and consistency.

A word of caution here: if you are only ever focused on coaching the business, you will not win the long-term loyalty of your team. Showing a softer, more vulnerable side is important, along with genuinely caring about the people on your team. The business does not have feelings, but everything that makes it run, does. And the emotional and psychological connections you make will give you the right to hold people accountable, as well as the permission to have the harder conversations when needed. Trying to have direct conversations with someone you barely know outside of their job function is the surest way to get them to shut down when you try to hold them accountable, and your recognition will not have the desired impact. It will be seen as a box being checked, something that you must do because you're told to do it. Don't be that manager. Every single person who has ever been in sales knows two stories- The Leader they strive to be like and The Cautionary Tale to avoid at all costs. No one wants to be the latter. Because trust me when I tell you that in a sales environment, your reputation will precede you. Be intentional about creating your image. Be fair and consistent. If you can't be fair, just be consistent. People will respect you even if they don't like you. Let that sink in for a bit.

I've had hundreds of reps who would never want to take me out for a beer, but they would've loved to be on my team. They knew me to be tough but consistent. And my teams always ranked in the top across the country. I share this not to brag, but rather as a testament to the power of accountability.

Discipline

Discipline is one of the most misused words in a manager's vocabulary. It is often confused with punishment or carries a negative connotation. Rather than being used as a stick to beat up underperforming reps, it should be used as its primary definition, an orderly or prescribed pattern of behavior. Think about it this way; if a doctor prescribes you antibiotics, you do not view that as punitive. Rather, it is an orderly process to achieve a desired result. Take this pill twice daily with food for 2 weeks or until gone. There is nothing disciplinary about that. The same goes for any activity which we seek to master, or at least become skilled at. I have often said to people that discipline is what will carry you after motivation wanes. Falling back to an orderly process as a means to achieve your end goal. The concept is simple, but only those who continue to execute will actually win. Think of athletes, writers, artists, musicians, and sculptors. They all encounter setbacks, competition, and problems, but those that have the discipline to practice or continue to hone their craft become the ones we read about. All the others fall off and are swept into the dustbin of history. I am one such person.

You see, long ago, I had a desire to become a great painter. I loved the idea and romanticized the notion that I could be like Davinci,

Rembrandt, Renoir, all of them. I never achieved that for several reasons. One was a lack of discipline. Once I ran into a few minor setbacks, I put it all down and never picked it back up. Now, truth be told, I never really had the basic skills to become an actual artist, but that's a moot point. My motivation faded with time and focus, and without the discipline to persevere, it was over before it really started.

We do this all too often to others. Instead of teaching them to use obstacles, problems, and challenges to fuel their desire, we let it act like a candle lid and extinguish the flame that was in their heart. In order to help others to build and sharpen their discipline, we must first understand how to wield such a powerful tool.

Most highly successful people have areas of their lives where they employ extreme discipline. This is not accidental, but rather quite intentional. In order to achieve big goals or to maintain focus on long-term ideas, discipline is required. No one can stay on track to make a million dollars year after year without the discipline to stay the course. Unless of course, you figure out how to win the Powerball annually. In which case it could be argued that you're simply extremely lucky. Business is not all that dissimilar to athletic competitions. You plan your training or strategy and then spend the next year executing and correcting course when needed. If either the athlete or the business leader stops working their plan, things will undoubtedly veer off course. Not only does that stall your business or your fitness, you'll also spend quite a bit of time getting back to where you were. That whiplash of sorts is very tough on your body and your business. In fact, more employees will become frustrated or leave an organization if the leadership cannot maintain a consistent strategy. Constantly changing directions means that you didn't plan accordingly, or you've failed in true execution of the plan. Re-prioritizing your priorities should only happen in the case of material change to market conditions, customer base, or some unforeseen internal change, and should only be a last resort. I can cite numerous examples of companies falling into "flavor of the month" strategizing and how that ultimately did not work in their favor. Now, that does not mean that you go the way of Blockbuster or Circuit City and simply refuse to read the writing on the wall, but if you constantly change for the sake of change, you will burn out your employees and bog down front-line leaders. Neither of these are practices that will help to move your business forward.

Now having discussed what discipline is and the need for it, let's dig into the methods to use in order to build a stronger business and create higher performing teams. As a sales or business leader, you should always be looking for ways to lead by example. Simply believing that younger employees or less experienced ones will suddenly and miraculously figure it out on their own is not an effective strategy. Your approach should always follow the time-tested tell, show, watch, format. First, you explain what to do. Then you show how to correctly execute, and finally, you watch them try it on their own. You can offer encouragement or gentle correction, but it's usually not a bad idea to allow them to fail on the first few attempts.

In order to truly lead by example, you must learn to consistently and effectively leverage discipline. Creating a morning routine that you maintain is a great first start. Blocking time on your calendar so that others do not manage your time can help prevent burnout or frustration that comes with rushing from meeting to meeting. Recurring meetings with no agenda or defined action items tend to be some of the most colossal time drains, yet for some people, the comfort of having those meetings is all the justification they need to clog your calendar and deprive you of managing your week.

A good morning routine is something that all business and especially sales leaders should look to create. It allows for important tasks to not get missed and sets the tone for each day. Before everyone reading this throws up their hands and says that they "aren't a morning person," I'd ask you to hear me out. My morning routine focuses specifically on spirit, soul, and body. Morning rituals have long been associated with success and high performance, because they help to align your focus and adequately prepare for the day. How many times do you hear people say that their mornings leave them feeling scattered and ungrounded? What's more, is those people then show up at your business to offload all that negative energy and chaos. If you have team members or colleagues who are seemingly eternally late, rushed, and a virtual train wreck, you may want to schedule an intervention. Otherwise, how could they possibly be contributing members to your organization? Odds are they don't get a grasp on things until lunchtime, meaning that they have neither the time or the ability to prepare for meetings and projects. Add in meetings about meetings where you discuss the next meeting, and you can easily see why so many companies are bereft with problems, confusion, and inefficiencies.

The earlier you get up, the better, but this should not be the case if you work third shift or something like that. The general framework is one you can apply, regardless of the time of day. My basic routine is outlined here, though it does allow for flexibility based on travel and other circumstances.

4:30-5:00 Wake up (timing can be much earlier on travel days or slightly later if on vacation)

5:30-6:30 Make coffee and meditate, journal, and organize for the day (this is time to reflect and set intentions for the day. I prefer to be outside on the deck or patio at this time)

6:30-8:00 Work out (I usually make this workout about strength and mobility, saving a run for lunchtime or evening)

8:00-9:00 Check emails, review schedule

From here, my day is run mostly by my calendar. And since I spend a few minutes early in the day reviewing that schedule, I can make changes as needed or add other things to it. Don't be afraid to add personal appointments or time to work on specific things. Remember, it's your calendar and schedule. There will always be fires to put out or meetings that pop up throughout the week but maintaining discipline of HOW you start your day is the key. If you don't take control of your daily schedule, others or events will. And there is nothing that causes a sense of lack of control like losing complete governance of your day. Keep in mind that it will happen, but it must be the ultra-rare exception, not the rule. I would also point out that the first several hours of my day are focused selfishly on my own improvement. That is absolutely by design. You cannot mentor, coach, or guide others if you are a hot mess. Too many leaders think that bursting into the office all frazzled and creating a whirlwind of chaos until you leave is the sign of an eccentric genius. It may be, but unless your IQ is over 135, you're not in the 99th percentile to refer to yourself as a brainiac. Organization and optimization are far better indicators of intelligence than chaos and confusion. As Gen. Robert H. Barrow so aptly put it, "Amateurs talk about tactics, but professionals study logistics." Focusing only on what you are going to do and not on how to sustain and consistently deliver has been the demise of many a sales leader. If you are always late to meetings, habitually unprepared, you will only deliver chaos and confusion. Organization allows you to see down the road and think 3 steps ahead. Optimization means you are flexible and adaptable. You cannot be the latter if you are operating constantly on the fly.

The next thing many people say after reading this is that they don't like to work out in the morning. No kidding, most people don't. I do not. At least not most days. In fact, for years I tried to keep my workout to the evenings. What I found was that it wasn't a quality workout after the stress of the day had zapped my energy and time. I switched to working out first thing in the morning, and despite not really enjoying it when I start, by the end I feel a thousand times better. It's the first in a series of stacked wins that builds momentum. Obviously, this is a bit of psychological warfare on yourself, and that is just fine. I promise you that when it's cold and dark outside, or when frigid winter temperatures hit, crawling out of a warm bed is NOT the first and best idea. This is precisely where discipline will come in. If we allowed how we feel to run our day, not a damn thing would get accomplished on time. Feel free to attempt to prove me wrong, it's your life that you'll throw into disarray, not mine.

Getting back to the selfish nature of my morning routine, I call this out because it's true. You need to spend time focusing on improving yourself before you can help others to do the same. Even the airlines recognize this and direct you to put your oxygen mask on first before helping other passengers in the event that there's a loss of cabin pressure.

As with everything, there are exceptions to this routine. If you are ill or injured, you need time to recover and you can't just keep going for runs if you sprain an ankle. Be smart about it. Discipline does not equate to ego. In fact, it pretty much overpowers ego. It's really difficult to take all the credit for success when the only way you realize it is to have a very disciplined approach. By following predetermined steps, you replace hubris with humility.

Attention

In today's modern, fast-paced world, your attention is being grabbed by each and every ad, device, program, you name it. In fact, there are few times and even fewer places you can go to get away from the attention suck of today's business world. I try to unsubscribe from no less than 3 email campaigns per day. Why? Because I only have so many hours in the day and I drive my schedule. I am the one who should decide what goods or services I purchase because I need them, not because someone serves up a good deal.

I heard a quote the other day on a podcast that you should pay attention, not give it. In my opinion, social media is one of the absolute worst offenders. It's literally designed to take your time. Not in the sense of slowing down, but literally taking your time away from other things, tasks, and people. If you think about it, the approach and concept is quite insidious. We begin to unconsciously scroll through pictures and videos, weighing in on arguments without any true merit, all day long. For hours, people will consume content that has no positive impact on their day and then wonder why they accomplished nothing. Those that learn to carve out time for that activity tend to fall into the time trap less, but it still has the potential to derail their day. Now, I'm not saying to avoid any and all communications or programs, but where you focus your energy is where you will grow. If you spend hours looking at what other people are saying or doing, how exactly does that improve your life? Sure, we can get inspiration or zone out for a bit, but that cannot be your main focus or you'll never have time to do the things you need to in order to edify your own spirit, soul, and body. Not to mention all the negativity and vitriol that has overtaken most social media or the comments on the news sites. Instead of wasting hours being dragged down with the keyboard warriors, spend an extra 15 minutes getting quiet and work through a problem with your business. Or invent something new. Go for a walk. Drink more water. Any and all of these things will boost your psyche and put you in a position to win.

Going back to your morning routine, every business leader, regardless of their title, should set time to intentionally improve their team or their business. Every organization sets goals for the month, the quarter, and the year. Virtually everyone has a revenue goal, and probably some sort of client or customer-based goal. Years ago, I started carrying hard cover journals to take notes and plan with. Inside the cover, I would write 4 questions that I should be able to answer. At the beginning of the day, I would read them and incorporate them into my day and then review them to confirm that I did in fact accomplish them at the close of each day. After a while, it simply became part of my daily routine and my attention shifted. I now have 4 goals or questions for myself every day.

Today have I:

1. Done something to create a robust sales culture?
2. Shown myself as an innovative sales leader?
3. Empowered someone to run their business?
4. Noticed the cast of my leadership shadow?

I can assure you, there were and are days when I don't accomplish all 4 goals. Some days, it's a struggle to do just one. However, I believe that the universe appreciates and rewards right intention. Looking over that list even many years after adopting them, I cannot find any reason to change them. I have no illusion that these same 4 questions will work perfect for everyone, so feel free to change them as you need to in order to have a positive impact on your life and business.

Digging in to the 4 questions, I want to further explore each as it pertains specifically to sales leadership. As we unpack each of the items, I encourage you to put them into your own words or use them verbatim. Whatever works for you, as I do not own the rights to them.

Have I done something to create a robust sales culture?

What is a robust sales culture, and how does anyone create it? This book is set up intentionally to walk sales and business leaders down the path of self-discovery. That said, the first three chapters encompass a robust sales culture. You hire slowly and methodically. You learn to visualize what a sales rep can grow into, what their true potential is. So, something that you might do to create a robust sales culture may be as simple as having a conversation with an attentive server at a restaurant, outlining a sales contest for your team, or simply working with your hiring staff to refine who your ideal candidate would be. All these activities work toward creating a positive, competitive, and focused team. Thus, the very definition of robust sales culture.

Have I shown myself as an innovative sales leader?

This one can be a little less straightforward at first, though once you get the hang of it, the concept will make complete sense. What is an innovative sales leader? It's someone who recognizes their strengths and plays to them. But they also play to the strengths of others. One way I used to do this is by pairing projects or tasks with strengths. I had one manager who was absolutely a master with Excel. He would be tasked with all of our spreadsheet and reporting needs. I had another manager that could break any Excel spreadsheet within seconds of receiving it, so she wasn't tasked with working within the program. She did, however, have an incredible ability to negotiate virtually everything. And she would undoubtedly come out on top. She and one of her colleagues, who was also a manager of mine, were astonishingly creative when it came to creating sales contests. They knew what drove their teams and leveraged that. It is no secret that we only have so many hours in the day, and the best and most innovative sales leaders don't come up with every idea on their own. They learn from other's success and failure, and there have been endless books written about those experiences (not unlike this one). Reading gives you the cliff's notes version, distilling years of trial and error into an easy-to-follow format. Never underestimate the power of books.

Have I empowered someone to run their business?

The third question is arguably the most difficult for young leaders to implement. This is mostly due to the fact that it requires, in the strictest of terms, that you cede control of an activity or situation, knowing full well that there is an above average chance that the rep will fail. Not only must you accept this risk but embrace it and learn to be ok with it. Read that again. Yes, I am literally saying that there will be times when you must allow your team to screw things up the way only a salesperson can. And not just allow it but encourage it. This is how they learn, grow, and become innovative as well as help you create a robust sales culture. It's a tough pill to swallow, especially when your compensation is tied to the results your teams produce. However, if you do this early and often, you should not find yourself in the position where everyone is destroying your business at the same time. There also may come a time when you have to determine that someone isn't comfortable with failing, and they may not be a good fit. We'll discuss that in the next chapter. Keep in mind that no one learns anything new without failing first. Thomas Edison is famous for saying that he never failed but found 10,000 ways to not make a lightbulb. It does not take a linguist to understand that he was saying "I messed up a lot before I found success." Learning how to strategically allow your team to fail and not just fail but figure out how to iterate, is the hallmark of a strong leader.

One of my favorite quotes of all time comes from Lao Tzu- *"To lead people, walk behind them."* In essence, you give up control but display confidence. You can quietly clean up when needed but allowing your team an open view of the world empowers them to do great things.

Have I noticed the cast of my leadership shadow?

This one is an exercise in humility. I posit that most of the problems we as leaders see with our teams are our own fault. Much the same, our success is because we pushed the right way and focused on the right things. Years after writing this question, I learned about shadow work. It's a pretty complex sociological phenomenon, but it can be stated as recognizing a past version of ourselves in others and their actions. Think of that the next time one of your reps does something that angers you. Was it something that you've done in the past? Was it something that happened before, and you didn't address it? I hate to tell you this, but most of those things are your fault. It sounds callous, but you're the leader. Maybe it's a rep who is habitually late. It drives you nuts because your boss used to always be late to your coaching sessions. Or maybe your parent or spouse can never be on time. In any case, it's something that you've not resolved in your own life or past and is rearing its ugly head again. Conversely, when we celebrate someone or their success, it's because those are traits and characteristics that we want and have. You were put in a position of leadership for a reason, and liking victory is not a bad thing. But it comes from your guidance and focus helping them get there.

The concept of shadow work is really deep. The worst part about it is that it forces us as leaders to look in the mirror even more than we already do. I cannot think of any sales or business leader who is successful and who doesn't have more than their fair share of self-criticisms. As salespeople, the world often thinks we're cocky know-it-alls, when in reality we tend to be our harshest critics 23 out of every 24 hours. By asking yourself if you noticed the cast of your leadership shadow, you are also giving yourself permission to celebrate. To focus on the wins no matter how small. To recognize all the sweat, tears, and often blood we pour into our teams. We're immeasurably invested in our people. If you aren't it may be time to rethink your career.

Change the People or
Change the People

As leaders, we often inherit teams or people on our teams. As our businesses grow and evolve, sometimes the members of our teams do not. Either they cannot adapt to changing circumstances, the environment, the market, or another contributing factor. Oftentimes it comes across as having a stable full of legless horses. Fortunately, that's usually just perception and not reality. In any case, and more often than you'd like, you will be faced with a challenging rep. To protect the innocent and the guilty, I will not use any names as I describe two situations. You can put names to them to fit your own current or past challenges.

Scenario 1 – You've just relocated to a new state and a new office. Having been a manager for less than a year, and now in a totally new environment, you obviously want to stack a few wins with your new team. Every day, one rep darkens your doorway. X has not shown himself to be particularly strong from a sales perspective and you always get the impression that he is sizing you up to see how he can manipulate you. Even as a young manager, your instincts tell you to give him the benefit of the doubt and let him feel out your leadership style. Every time the rep comes to your office, X has a complaint that someone else is doing something they shouldn't be. One day it's talking too loudly on their calls, the next it's overinflating their opportunities. Your first inclination is to simply tell him to go back to his desk and focus on his customers. Instead, you decide to do some investigating.

Here's a bit of time-tested advice; spend time on the floor every single day. Nothing sanitizes a sales floor like a manager actively engaged in the selling process. You'll be able to see firsthand what and who is working and what and who is not. So, that's exactly what I did. I would spend 15-30 minutes at each desk throughout the week, rolling my chair and headset up and plugging in to listen to calls, live. I immediately learned who was working and selling versus who was trying to run out the clock. I noticed that X was conspicuously absent from his desk more often than sitting at it working. Rather than track him down in the building, I upped the ante. I started pulling random calls and scheduled time for 2 reps at a time to join me in reviewing these calls. I tried to pick reps that didn't sit near each other so that they could hear another perspective and maybe pick something up that would help them.

After a few weeks of these two exercises, X was the only one who always had an excuse or would push back on having his calls played for a peer. Don't get me wrong, it was uncomfortable for every one of them initially, but after a few repetitions, they started asking for those sessions! Wonders never cease! Well, after a few more days of observation, I waited until X came to complain about something. He must have anticipated that the trap had been set, because the complaint on that day was a very serious allegation. Instead of moving to directly address it, I had him close the door and sit down. Pulling a page from *Crucial Conversations*, I began by laying out what I had seen and observed over the last few weeks. I closed by telling him that it was clear that he was the issue because he was focused on everything but his actual job. I told him I wanted him to go back to his desk and I wanted to confer with my Director about next steps.

Wouldn't you know it, the very next day he came to me to ask about a transfer to another team. He really thought he was better suited to sell a particular line of business than manage contract customers. I played it off as though I would have to think about it, but only to hide the fact that I was whipping out my pen to sign off on the transfer in seconds! In the end, X did transfer. And not long after that, X was having the same issues, but now was always wandering around the building talking on his cell phone instead of calling customers. It took another year or so but X was eventually let go. I never learned the reasoning, and candidly, I didn't care. I may have pawned off my problem of the moment, but I gave as transparent of feedback to the new manager as I could. Either way, I changed the person. Sometimes managing people is more about playing chess than it is about checkers.

Scenario 2 – While quite different from Scenario 1, it still worked out better than I could have ever imagined. After about a year in that role, a position opened at the same level, however it would be managing a team that worked West Coast hours. I had been part of a pilot group as a rep working that schedule, so it wasn't too foreign by any means. It did mean that I would have to take on a totally new team, one that due to other circumstances had been without a manager for some time. This new team had a lot working against them. Their manager was under investigation and ultimately resigned. They worked odd hours and were tucked away in a different part of the building. Many of the reps were new to sales and had virtually no coaching. I knew I would have my hands full, but I was emboldened by being able to get my previous team turned around to the point where I won the equivalent of President's Club.

Taking on this new band of misfits, I immediately started spending hours a day on the floor in their cubes with them listening to calls, talking to customers, and being uber visible and engaged. One rep on the team was a very nice young woman. She was high energy, very relatable, and genuinely welcoming to everything, except me sitting with her and listening to calls live.

When it came time for me to sit with her the first time, I tried to put her at ease by letting her know I was just listening, and it was more to hear from her customers than anything else. Truth be told, that was a lie, but what manager hasn't bent the truth to coach?

Perhaps I am the only one. Regardless, she dials her first customer and I had inadvertently changed the position of the switch so the other end couldn't hear her. Imagine the scene of this young woman, so far outside her comfort zone, and now immensely embarrassed. I got to spend the next several minutes trying to keep her from hyperventilating. Eventually, we go it figured out and she had some really good calls. Each session was a bit of a bear to get started, but she was becoming a very strong rep.

This story has a very different ending than the last. She went on to not only become more of a mentor but was in fact promoted to manager herself a few years later. Rumor has it she's still doing great things. While it was uncomfortable and challenging, she changed and grew as a professional. That was a proud moment.

People only change their perspective or position when they are forced to. No one likes to change, despite the numerous quotes, essays, and inspirational posters being created that say otherwise. One of the most important questions a sales leader should ask on a regular basis is: "Are the right people in the right seats?" Having the right person in the right role is the secret sauce. Not everyone will excel or thrive in every role in the organization. Therefore, creating the right environment and culture, holding people accountable and fostering discipline are crucial to shaping a high performing team and organization. Without these steps securely in place, sales leaders will find themselves playing management by whack-a-mole instead of leading a hard charging team that continues to raise the bar.

The main critique I have received around the concept of change the people or change the people is that it is far too binary of a response. To the uninitiated, yes, it could be. However, this is simply one step in a process. Again, if you have effectively held your people accountable in the correct environment, and worked to maintain discipline, then you should not need to fire like it is a bodily function. Instead, this cycle of hiring slowly to a defined profile, combined with consistent and disciplined coaching, should result in employees at all levels finding their true path. Thus, the need to fire will remain reserved for cause. In the next chapter, we'll tackle the hiring process.

Hire Slowly, Fire Quickly

Nearly every manager has heard the phrase, yet nearly every manager has an excuse as to why it "doesn't fit" in their organization. This is especially true when they know they've made a bad hire. So why do managers make poor hiring decisions? Look, we've all done it. And in hindsight, you can look back and there was probably a moment very early on that gave you pause, or something seemed "off" about the candidate. But you had an open book, customers that needed to be served, or maybe you were just tired of filling in as pseudo customer service. Any way you slice it, you screwed up. Odds are, you know it, your boss knows it, even the employee in question probably knows it. So why do they stay? There could be one or multiple reasons; it's easier to look for a job when you have one, insurance or retirement is the perk they were looking for, or some people just continually game the system. They pour their energy into staying one step ahead so that they feel like they have control.

Let's break this down into distinct steps of the process, and hopefully you can reduce the number of times you are faced with this unpleasant situation.

1. Pre-Interview

2. Interview
3. First 90 days
4. Career Pathing

You may have a completely different methodology to this, and if that is working for you, great. I say keep it going, but make sure you are open to improving or pivoting when needed. Nothing should be rigid about the hiring process other than consistency. After all, you want to steer clear of lawsuits.

The Pre-Interview stage is where you develop the hiring profile, job description, and understand the current job market and candidate pool in your area. This is where you define the purpose of hiring, who your ideal candidate is, and what resources you need in order to make them and the organization successful.

The size of your company usually dictates how involved the hiring manager is at this point. In working in corporate America, there were teams involved in this. Working at a small, less than 10-person company, I spent hours working and re-working job descriptions, figuring out how to fund the role, and aligning with our growth plans. This can successfully be outsourced, however, there will be an expense associated with it. I'd recommend that you handle it personally for as long as it makes sense. The challenge here, is that the smaller the organization, the more impactful the decisions you make will be. The wrong hire in a company of 8 can set you back years. The wrong hire in a company of 25,000 will likely never be noticed beyond direct peers.

Writing job descriptions is akin to making a Christmas list. It's everything you dream about someone taking on for you. The job description and the hiring profile should be an iterative process and getting more than one set of eyes on it will only serve to narrow the scope and clarify the role. As a highly visual person, I like to whiteboard this step and align with a printout of the desired future organizational chart. Side note, if you do not have multiple versions of an org chart, start there. It will not only help every other process in the people management side but will also help keep your vision alive. Make them. Draw them up on napkins, put them in Excel, however you work, use that. If you are President of a small company, share these often with your trusted inner circle. Your right hand needs to know where to steer the ship. The basic rule of thumb here is anyone who sees your P&L (the unedited, unredacted version) and participates in budget setting, or is VP level or above, needs to have at a minimum a working understanding of where you want to go.

Many years ago, I sat in on a weeklong planning session with 2 dozen other Directors, VPs, and the occasional senior execs. The fiscal year had just started, and the discussions around headcount, expenses, and human capital were in full swing. At one point, I asked my direct supervisor when we could sit down and review the budget for our department. The response was swift and final.

"You don't need to see that. You don't make any decisions that would impact it." Ouch. Talk about deflating your team. Mind you, at that time, my teams handled just south of $400 million in business. Instead of using it as an opportunity to gain trust and bring a Director behind the curtain, I was told in no uncertain terms that my influence was fictional. Got it. I'll let you guess as to what my relationship with that individual was like after this interaction. Spoiler alert-I would've rather have a dentist's drill as an alarm clock than ever give them an ounce of respect. In fact, on the very same trip, I was stuck with a $400 bar bill from all the fat cats and hangers on so their boss wouldn't see it. Dirty politics at its finest. But I digress.

Once you have job descriptions aligned with the org chart and your vision, you need to create the hiring profile and the interview guides simultaneously. How can you interview someone if you don't know WHO you are looking for? Don't be afraid to start by being very broad and vague here, but make sure you get down to where any hiring manager can spot the ideal candidate in a crowd. A lot of how this plays out will be determined by how your teams are structured and the number and scope of the roles that comprise your team or department. However, transparency and communication with your hiring managers up and down and across the company will make you more nimble, innovative, and able to move much quicker than organizations with layer upon layer of bureaucracy. Your pre-interview stage helps you set the framework and foundation for hiring the best possible candidates.

Bringing your front-line managers and hiring managers into the process will serve you many times over.

The interview phase is where you implement the interview guide and go through the process of meeting with candidates. A word of caution here, do not interview any and everyone who applies. Whether you are an entrepreneur just starting a company, or the CEO of a Fortune 100 company, your time has more value than you think. Pre-screening is a must. Develop a rhythm to the process. At the end of each day or week, review those who have applied. Understand their background and do some research into those who pique your interest. Focus on transferable skills in addition to verifiable experience. Look for gaps in employment or job hopping. These should not immediately disqualify someone but should be points of discussion. Also, take note if the candidate broaches the subject if you have a possible red flag, or if you must pry the context out of them.

Unfortunately, every human has unconscious bias that are formed based on their experiences in and out of a professional setting. That means you will have to acknowledge your bias if they attended a particular school, grew up in a rough part of town, or any number of other factors. Too often quality candidates are passed over because a hiring manager cannot approach the interview with an open mind. We're all guilty of it, despite how empathetic we envision ourselves to be.

Once you have several candidates, begin interviewing. If you have not developed an interview summary checklist that will allow you to quickly compile the main points and how the candidate responds, do so before you start interviewing. This not only provides consistency in how you evaluate candidates but helps to jog your memory after asking the same questions 200 times. Who had responses that stood out, for good or bad reasons? Who was late? Who wrote a thank you card? Who showed up looking like they'd just rolled out of bed? These are all things that will run together in your memory and a summary checklist can help keep the top candidates at the forefront. Now for what's always the hardest part for everyone to understand; if you don't immediately find the candidate to be a "yes" or they would not be well-suited for another role, ***DO NOT HIRE THEM***.

No matter how badly you want the seat filled. You will regret it. I cannot tell you how many times I have had hiring managers say "I really liked Tom, but Jen wasn't bad. I don't want to decline Jen in case Tom doesn't accept." It's a very logical thought process, but hiring the right candidate isn't always logical. When you are at the car dealership looking at a car, you never take a second look at a vehicle once you have test driven "the one." Hiring good people is no different. A yes is a yes and a no is a no. Coach your hiring managers that this is non-negotiable. If you don't have time to leave a book of business open, then you certainly won't have time to maybe, possibly, get someone up to speed. And you certainly will not have time to repeatedly interview and hire for the same position because you keep forcing someone to be a good fit. Front line managers and those with responsibility for revenue should not be focused on pet projects. It sounds callous, but I have yet to see a sales leader who can juggle top performers and someone who could be good at some point.

Once you have identified the top candidates, make time to review everyone one more time with the hiring managers. This will likely be a robust conversation, as everyone will have their "favorite" for their team. As the leader, your job is to keep the dialogue revenue-centered, objective, and success focused. That means that it does not matter than Susie had bright blue hair, or that Jimmy is a Cowboys fan. If they met the basic criteria and made it to the interview, responded well during the interview, and made their way to the top of the interviewed candidates, you have yourself a new hire. The reason I structured the process to have so many steps to get to an offer being extended, is to ensure that you are removing all unconscious and conscious bias. Trust the process yourself, and coach your managers to trust the process as well.

The first 90 days of any role will begin to define the level of success a person will achieve. I can't tell you how many times we had someone make it through the screening process, nail the interview, and on day one starts acting like they own the company. They show up late, leave early, have 15 grandmas that suddenly and inexplicably pass away at the most convenient times. That is why you must call out the probationary period and make sure you are documenting and creating a paper trail. These notes, 30/60/90-day reviews will not only help you determine whether or not the employee should stay, but can also help you with step 4, career pathing. Keeping this in mind, if you have a manager who wants to avoid the difficult conversations and you are approaching the 90-day mark, you have one of two options as the leader. You can either let them take complete ownership and let them know you will not hold back on the "I told you so" when they inevitably don't work out, or you can stay close to the development process with your manager and guide them through it. You should only have to be heavily involved a few times before they start to understand what to look for and what not to tolerate. Also, provided you are consistently coaching and developing your managers, you'll have most of the groundwork laid.

Your sales managers cannot avoid having tough conversations. They should not be caustic or always looking for conflict, but they should not shy away from it either. Conflict is absolutely guaranteed and is often extremely healthy. There is a large segment of the population that believes everyone should present a plan for their first 90 days in their new role. I happen to like them, as it gives insight into how the employee or candidate plans, and if it contains commitments, you can use that as part of your coaching if they align with your strategy. For example, if they put into their presentation that they will be extremely responsive to customers as part of their role, then getting multiple complaints that they haven't and do not respond in a timely manner is a very direct point for coaching. What most leaders don't want to admit is that a 90-day plan is not the most useful of things a new hire can do. Especially if they are new to the organization or industry. Far too many plans end up in the trash instead of being refined and treated as a living document. Try not to get caught up in the details in the plan, but rather focus on how they built it. No plan should be so rigid and strict. However, the ability of a new hire to think critically about the position and how they approach it will tell you if they have what it takes to be a leader in due time.

Career pathing has become a buzzword, yet far too few companies fully understand how to design, implement, and execute such an employee specific process. It is also more complicated than just asking someone what they want to do in their career. Career paths can and should be aligned to both your current and future state organizational charts. They should, arguably, assist in moving the entire company or division from its current state to the future state via promotion and growth. Gone should be the days of creating roles and titles just to have them. They should be conduits for development and promotions should be the result of growth and consistent results. Under no circumstances should promotions be based on entitlement or length of time in a role. I used to have reps come into my office and want to talk about how to get promoted to a manager level. It was exhausting, mostly because nearly everyone hadn't been in their role more than a few months. If they had been there longer, their production was nothing to write home about. But they had seen others get promoted who they didn't feel deserved it, so they figured if Billy could be a manager, why couldn't they? Besides, managers made a lot more money.

Like the other steps in the hiring process, leaders should formalize as many aspects of building a career path as possible. While each company and industry will likely have their unique steps, that does not preclude introducing young employees to the complexities of people management.

When an employee would set time with me, the first thing I would tell them as they took a seat in my office was this: your interview hasn't stopped since you were hired, and it will not stop until you leave the company or retire. I can't speak for my colleagues in the company at the time, but I was always watching. I paid attention to how employees interacted with their customers and peers, as well as how they dressed and presented themselves in meetings and trainings.

One of my favorite tasks I would assign to anyone who wanted to get promoted was fairly simple, but it really forced them to think outside the box of what they had control over. After speaking with them to get some context on their background and experience, I would send them away with homework. They would be instructed to stack rank their team, including themselves. When we would get back together, I wanted to hear why they ranked everyone where they did, and then the next piece of homework was to develop the plan on how they would help get the lower ranked individuals to improve.

I initially caught a lot of grumbling for this exercise, but it clearly showed me several very important things. First, it became very obvious how they viewed their own performance when compared to their peers. In fact, it was not all that different than watching someone look in the mirror and voice their insecurities. I wanted to know if they had the emotional intelligence and self-awareness to be able to compare themselves to their peers. It sounds silly and simple, yet it is extremely uncomfortable for some. The second thing it showed was their willingness to be open and transparent with the Director level. If they were only confident in gossiping with peers versus strategizing with a leader, they most likely couldn't keep confidential information to their own heads. The third and most important result of the exercise was if they had the ability to understand where and how to develop others. But not just anyone. Since the ranking and planning was done on their own team, I wanted to see how they could transition, at least in theory, from a peer to a leader. This is arguably one of the most difficult transitions for employees to make, and where many get caught unable to leave their old world behind.

I would also have the same employee build a 90-day plan to outline their first quarter as a manager for a fictitious team. You'd be shocked to know just how many were so focused on "driving results" yet couldn't be bothered to implement those same tactics in their current role. It should come as no surprise that many of these conversations fizzled out after one or two meetings. But I knew that if I made it easy and convinced them that the job would always be rainbows and unicorns, I would be doing everyone a disservice.

Virtually everyone wants to be promoted. They like the compensation, the prestige, the travel, all of the cool parts of leadership. What they don't see and don't want to talk about are the long days, longer hours, travel exhaustion, being everyone's emotional punching bag, acting as a therapist, the pain of having to make difficult decisions, and the frustration caused by employee immaturity. The list goes on. I made a very specific point of asking over and over why they wanted to do this. I would have them talk to recently promoted managers in addition to tenured ones. Without hesitation, every manager would tell them that it was very different than they thought it would be. Greener grass and all.

At the end of all this, if they made the effort to complete their evaluation and improved their own position, I rarely had the opportunity to hire them. Someone else usually did or they ended up leaving to go work somewhere else. I have never regretted accepting a resignation letter or wishing someone best of luck elsewhere. Working on my team and for me, was tough. That was widely known. I only recall ever raising my voice once and while justified, it was not appropriate and I quickly apologized.

Creating a career path for employees is not an event. Rather, it is a process that ebbs and flows. It takes patience and focus, from all parties involved. Having strong, clear processes and proven success in getting people to the next level can help to reduce or nearly eliminate the political nonsense that infects organizations at all levels. Companies that have clearly defined paths also tend to be more innovative. By working to employees' strengths, they often outrun their competitors because they have more people working on projects and failing fast.

One final thought on developing a career path; don't put all your eggs in one basket. If you only work with one employee to develop to the next level, you are only asking for problems. Keep in mind that when someone truly starts to envision their future, they can sometimes realize that while they can contribute in their current role, it isn't where their passion lies. In many cases, these rising stars can quickly become former employees as they set out to pursue something bigger. If you turn on the light in a room, be aware that some people will want to leave.

The final topic for this area is termination. This is the part of managing people that pretty much everyone dreads. Sure, many managers will toss the action around in conversation, but few really know how to terminate, much less when. Termination should follow one of three processes; for cause, performance based, or administrative.

Administrative termination is the simplest, so we can explain it quickly. This occurs primarily when someone gives their notice, they retire, or due to a reduction in force or elimination. Work with your HR department or professional consultant on any RIF within your company.

Termination for cause is quite broad, but you know it when it happens. Theft, job abandonment, tardiness, misuse of resources, fraud, creating a hostile work environment, and retaliation, all fall into this category. In nearly every case, it is incumbent on the leadership team that the issue is dealt with quickly and consistently. To allow things to be swept under the rug will not make situations better magically and will only serve to continue to erode trust and transparency. As unfortunate as it sounds, it is better to fire too quickly than too slowly.

Termination for performance can be challenging. Knowing when and how to let someone go because they are not performing to standard can easily become convoluted. Also, any time you do end up terminating for performance, you set the standard. That line in the sand is really difficult to move, so make sure that it is in fact the bare minimum you can tolerate. These guidelines should be set up long before you are put in a position to terminate and should never be negotiable. Word will get out faster than you can imagine, and you'll undoubtedly have a lawsuit on your hands.

As a general rule, documentation is key to performance management. Keeping record of one-on-one sessions in the form of recaps, developing a scorecard that sets the same standards for all sellers, as well as developing coaching templates will definitely keep you out of hot water. Again, creating the right culture will pay off in virtually every area of your business, and performance management is no exception.

How you process terminations will have a ripple effect in the organization. You absolutely never want to create an environment of fear, while at the same time being very clear about performance standards. You can be assured that you will have to deal with tears, insults, yelling, and the occasional physical altercation. Maintaining your cool and sticking to the facts without getting dragged down to the departing employee's level should remain top of mind. Any documentation, notes, counseling forms, etc. will be considered admissible in any lawsuit that result, so make sure that no company document contains commentary or opinions about the employee.

Documentation is a best practice for all areas of your business, except when it comes to your thoughts that come without context. For example, you should not write a note about how performance has dropped off because you believe that the divorce the employee is going through is impacting their ability to stay focused. The fact that performance has declined over time should be documented, however, the details regarding the employee's divorce should be left out, or kept vague, by including only that the employee may be managing personal matters outside of work that may be contributing to a decline in performance. That is factual and your thoughts around additional explanation are not out of line.

On the other hand, if you make a note that you overheard other employees discussing the fact that another employee put on weight and that is contributing to a loss in performance, you just set yourself up for a very nasty labor dispute. Please do not do this. Lawsuits for any company, but especially smaller organizations, have a devastating effect on everyone and every part of your business.

Coaching for Consistency

It has often been said that managing a business would be easier if it weren't for the burden of managing people. That is absolutely true. Effectively managing people is a constant pushing of rope. People do, say, and act in crazy ways at times. More often than not, it comes from some issue or circumstance outside of work, but nonetheless gets dragged into the office or workplace. And of course, this is on top of simply doing their jobs which only amplifies the need for coaching.

Quality coaching is an art form. It takes practice and consistency to be able to juggle job performance, social interaction, and disciplinary activities. To that end, coaching is conducted as one of three types: formal, developmental, and situational.

The first category of coaching is formal coaching. This is the scheduled, recurring, role specific type of conversation. Whether it is daily, weekly, monthly, or a combination thereof, these interactions are designed to help employees stay on track. During these sessions, the manager or leader will meet with an employee to review projects, tasks, and challenges that they are facing. It should be scheduled and follow the same agenda structure. By doing that, the employee and manager have less surprises and spend less time pulling things together. It allows for more focused dialogue and keeps both parties on task. If there are times when there may not be anything new to discuss, you can shorten the session or make it a bit less formal, but this should be the exception. The key is consistency and constantly canceling or moving the session around will not give you that consistency. Developing the same documentation, reporting, or scorecards for these sessions will assist in maintaining momentum and keep everyone focused on what is deemed important to the business. A best practice for these sessions is to have the employee recap in a very brief email to ensure that they correctly understood the content and have agreed upon next steps. When someone writes or types an idea, it becomes much more solid in their mind. It's far too easy to have details get forgotten or glossed over and the written recap will give both parties the opportunity to clarify or correct.

Developmental coaching is the second type of coaching session. This should follow a much longer cadence, and monthly is usually enough. These conversations center around growth and development, and tie directly into the career path discussions. Use these coaching sessions to work through reporting, create projects, read books, etc. so that the employee is working towards accelerating their skillset and focused on the bigger picture. While parts of these sessions will touch on role specific things, this should be a higher-level discussion and should include the previous year's annual review. For these, the leader or manager should be taking notes to continue the conversation between sessions, not all that dissimilar to the way a therapist works through issues with their clients. Developmental coaching sessions are designed for those who have achieved a level of success in their current role and have expressed the desire to do more. These are not effective or appropriate for new hires or for individuals who are not interested in moving up in the organization. Leave your worker bees to work.

Situational coaching is usually either disciplinary in nature or working through a very specific issue. These are not planned but should be recapped in an email or memo to file. DO NOT include personal details like medical information or anything, but do capture the material information such as date, time, issue or action that caused the coaching to be necessary. It should go without saying that this type of session should be infrequent. However, in the event that you find yourself having them with the same individuals, you will need to follow your disciplinary process to ensure that the root cause is being addressed.

The Five Types

Over the years, I have defined several personality types, or at least characters that inevitably seem to find their way into the workplace. To be clear, these traits are nowhere near official, but more designed to be used behind the scenes to know who you are dealing with. If they offend you, it's probably because you do not see yourself exhibiting the behaviors listed. The Five Types are as follows: The Historian, The Eternal Martyr, The Mother Hen, Eeyore, and the ubiquitous Emotional Responder.

Some employees have the unfortunate ability to move between these personalities, and worse yet, exhibit the majority of the behaviors. These personality types know no gender, ethnicity, age, or experience. They come from deeply held beliefs that generally have nothing to do with the business that you manage. The good news is that they can be coached into oblivion. Let's dig in.

The Historian can be incredibly frustrating. This individual always brings up the past. Think Uncle Rico from the movie *Napoleon Dynamite*. When they get into a situation where they are being held accountable, rest assured they will tell you about going to President's Club in 1987. They were at the top of their game. You just don't understand how they work. The Historian can be a challenge to work with, mostly because they dig their heels in the hardest when you are the most frustrated. The best thing you can do is put their storytelling on display. Allow them a few opportunities to start a rant in a group meeting and watch the eye rolls begin. In order to coach The Historian, you need to continually bring them back to the present. If something worked 30 years ago, try implementing it today. If it clearly does not work due to timing, relevance, or because you are in a different industry, you'll inch closer to showing them that the past should stay in the past. If it works, then more power to you. I would ask them to come up with the next idea to pilot. You will need to work on these individuals, and you will feel exhausted bouncing between the past and the present. That's ok, stack your wins and keep plugging along.

The Eternal Martyr is most frustrating to their peers. These employees always complain about how they go above and beyond. You read that correctly. If they have a pissed off client call them, the world needs to know how they got yelled at. They perceive everyone else as constantly slacking off and they take it upon themselves to ride in on their white horse and save the day. Then gripe about it. They are fun at office happy hours for about 10 minutes before you have to hear about how much harder they work than everyone else. They crave the attention and appreciation from leadership, but no one will give them more responsibility or a promotion because clearly, they are at their capacity. Instead of making it appear like they have mastered their role, their idea of job security is to tell anyone who will listen about how hard they have it. What they really have, is the exact wrong approach. Coaching them is going to be a deep dive into the realm of emotional intelligence. Buy them a book or two and have them read it and summarize it for you. Hold them accountable to working on their perception. Remind them daily to control what they can, and not focus on others unless specifically asked to. These employees are rarely approached to help others, because everyone knows that they will be made to feel indebted to The Martyr.

I had one associate who personified this personality to the letter. He was always working the hardest, the latest, and took on everyone else's responsibilities. He was habitually underpaid, and underappreciated, yet somehow never understood that most people wanted to leave him alone because obviously he had too much on his plate. Remember when George Costanza would walk around acting annoyed all the time to keep from getting more work? That is the very situation these individual's cause.

The Eeyore personality is self-explanatory but can still take on slight variations. These individuals are not easily excitable, which isn't in and of itself a bad thing, but cannot seem to find anything to celebrate. Everything should be done differently, but not by them. If there is a cloud in the sky, it's going to rain directly over them. And naturally, they will never carry an umbrella.

Mother Hen tends to be the least conflict-ridden personality. However, they can really stifle growth and innovation within your department or company. They need to check in incessantly on everyone around them and take on everyone's emotions. They focus on virtually everything that is out of their control and insert their overprotectiveness into the workplace. You can see what makes them so challenging. Salespeople need to be able to take calculated risks at work. Odds are many exhibit riskier behaviors outside of work, and while that doesn't concern you as the leader (provided they aren't breaking laws), it's all consuming to the Mother Hen. Watch their performance closely, because if they spend all their time worrying about others, your business will feel the impact.

The last and most challenging personality type is The Emotional Responder. Everything is a fire drill. All setbacks are catastrophic. Change of any kind is the end of the world. Flip side of the coin, if the vending machine in the breakroom has their favorite snack, they act like they cured cancer. Pop the champagne and let's have a party. With The Emotional Responder, you feel like you're constantly on a rollercoaster following their emotions, mainly getting a nasty case of whiplash. It is not a fun ride.

Virtually every office has named characters or personality types. The important takeaway here is not the names or the numbers of variations. Rather, managers and leaders should be cognizant if they have these individuals in their organization, who hired them, and whether or not their hiring process is capable of screening for problems before they are hired. Remember, these personality or character types are not inherently bad. In fact, most people will exhibit these behaviors from time to time in some fashion or another. What many do not realize is the damage to culture and focus and the havoc they can wreck in your business. If you spend all day trying to unravel he said/she said type issues, or you need to increase your budget for facial tissue to dry all the tears, you had better take a hard look at your hiring practices. Otherwise, all your focus and growth will be eroded by emotions and internal conversations. It is absolutely one of the most exhausting things a business leader can be forced to endure. Additionally, you will lose credibility with your staff if these items are not addressed consistently.

Be Fair and Consistent

Many years ago, I had a leader named Mike Zelenski who drilled this into my head. "Be fair and consistent." He is without a doubt one of the finest leaders I have ever served, and I would never have survived, much less thrived, without him. He was humble and could talk to anyone, but he always knew when to push and when to pull. At first, I felt like it was just another saying that some old timer came up with to sound smart. That was until I started to use it as a guiding principle. You've all been told that you can't please everyone all the time. That is correct. I would add that what is "fair" is incredibly subjective. Depending on the situation and your perspective, fair may be the furthest thing, especially if you are the recipient of anything you deem lesser than others. In other words, if the perceived benefit is not in your fair, the natural reaction of less mature minds is to call it unfair. I specifically call them less mature because as you experience life, you will begin to realize that the definition of "fair" is all about perception, not reality. Thus, be consistent. Consistency is a fact, an objective term. It merely means the same, unchanging. This also means that there will be times when you will need to make decisions that no one likes. That, unfortunately, is part of being a leader. Cleaning toilets in your house is not much fun, but it is required to live in a clean, sanitary home.

So how does a manager or leader create a culture where the employees embrace this line of thinking? Is it even possible to have an entire work force bought into the concept that decisions and actions will be fair and consistent? Or is that merely a pipe dream? The answer is that this is in fact possible, although it will require much discipline on the part of leadership. Culture is a lot like water. It will naturally seek out the path of least resistance, and always flows down. If your senior leadership team is not strictly disciplined in the hiring and coaching processes, then unfortunately very little of the visionary strategy will be adopted by those further removed from the top of the organization. Instead, sub-cultures will appear and morph, and these are often called cliques. Therefore, leadership defining and continually reinforcing the correct path is so important. Otherwise, managers especially, will find themselves managing by whack-a-mole. They will constantly be running around, putting out fires, consoling emotional responders, attempting to rewrite history for those who cannot leave it, trying to add some sunshine into the day for Eeyore, coddling the mother hen, and spending all day trying to reaffirm appreciation for the eternal martyr. Sounds exhausting, doesn't it? Perhaps that is why front-line managers tend to have such high turnover rates. They get burned out. Most weeks, the highlight of their job is a happy hour with their peers to have a few cocktails and commiserate with others who completely understand the level of excrement that gets flung at them. For you senior leaders, if your management team is always going to happy hour and you are never invited, you may want to do some digging into why. Now, do not expect to have an open invite. Your team needs and should absolutely have time to decompress and strategize sans supervision, but high performing teams will occasionally include their leaders. And this is not just so they can pick up the tab. Instead, it is an opportunity to loosen up a bit without having to close an office door or look over their shoulders to ensure that someone isn't listening to every word.

I used to take my managers out monthly, just to grab some drinks and appetizers. This time was used to help bring them closer together, but also to gain some insight into things that they discuss outside of work. You can often help resolve things before they become problems by addressing them in a more casual setting. Of course, it also affords you the opportunity to show your team that you aren't a complete stick in the mud. My favorite time with my managers were these days. And each year, I would take the team out for a nice dinner for the holidays. Yes, it cost me a few dollars. But few things were as important to them as breaking bread and sharing a few drinks all dressed up without needing to put on airs for anyone. It was an event that everyone looked forward to. I usually invited those who directly and strongly supported my teams, as a gesture of goodwill. I have to admit, though, that it caused a few waves around the building once word got out about what I did for my teams. Truthfully, I could not care any less. In fact, that was part of my master plan. To create so many layers to who I was as a leader, that no one could replicate it. A bit devious perhaps, though a lot of fun and extremely effective.

Acting fairly and consistently is most difficult at first for young leaders. But, as time progresses and that leader maintains the discipline of action and decision, it becomes part of their DNA. That is contagious to the employees, other leaders, and thus accelerates the right culture in your organization. The beauty of this is that even if you work for a large multi-national or global company, your division or department will always stand out. In fact, acting fair and consistent shows integrity, and adds another layer of strength to the team.

Skill or Will

This is a concept that is pretty straightforward. Skill means that someone may be lacking knowledge, experience, or training to help them excel in their current role. Will refers to their desire to work on areas where they are not strong. So, when we state that it is either skill or will, it's a shorter way of inquiring if the person has the tools to do the job or if they want to do the job. That's a very boiled down version of it, but it is quite a simple litmus test.

An example of each of these characteristics would be something along the lines of the scenarios below.

Sally had been in sales for the same company for nearly 20 years. She had won awards and accolades and her clients absolutely love her. Recently, her company implemented a new calendar software designed to make salespeople much more efficient in scheduling their days and weeks. Since it was based on very common concepts that are utilized in every university and college, the training was brief and to the point. Seemingly out of the blue, Sally began to see a decline in her production. Several complaints that she missed deadlines were escalated up to her manager. You spend a few weeks scratching your head, because for the last 3 years she's always been at the top. You meet with her manager and decide the best course of action is probably some casual observation. Maybe she's in a slump, or maybe she has just lost her edge. Either way, spending some extra time on the floor seems like a logical next step. Within hours, you identify the problem. She's having a hard time using the scheduling software, and the resulting frustration is causing her to panic and lose momentum.

You pull Sally into your office to have a frank conversation. She breaks down into tears, venting weeks of pent-up frustration in not being able to get the hang of using this new-fangled program. After much hand wringing behind closed doors, you get your answer by having a conversation with her. Together, you set time aside to help train her on the new program. Within days, her mood and production both improve. She's back to her old self, selling like a machine. In fact, Sally had the will all along, but lacked some basic training on an unfamiliar tool that became her biggest obstacle.

The frustration and embarrassment compiled to make for a rather tenuous situation. Had you not acted quickly, you may have made a very poor decision or coached Sally out of the role thinking that she was just ready to retire. This is a classic case of a skill issue. She had all the desire in the world to do the job, but she just needed a little boost with learning a new tool. Sales organizations are notorious for always looking for, buying, and botching the roll-out of new technology. There's a company that sells every conceivable gadget, plug in, snap on, widget and gizmo. Just because you get it doesn't mean that your people do. Take time to train them once, and you won't leave anyone behind.

Fred thought he was pretty cool. He was used to being the jock, the one everyone wanted to hang out with. When he landed a snazzy sales position, he came out of the gates like a prized thoroughbred. Within a few months, his complaints were outnumbering his revenue generated. When it came to team meetings, he became the loudmouth who always wanted to be paid more. His skillset demanded far more in compensation than he was making. He griped, grumbled, and spent more time trying to rally others behind his position than he did calling customers. It was exhausting.

Similar to Sally, you bring him in to get to the root of the problem. While he has a multitude of excuses, one thing becomes abundantly clear- he doesn't want to do the job. If you've never been a front-line seller, this may come as a surprise. But the day-to-day monotony can take its toll on the best salesperson. As mentioned earlier, extreme discipline is the only thing that will help carry salespeople through long, tiresome days. The lack of the desire to put in the work required is the classic example of a will issue. They have every tool and skill to do the job, but they get in their own way.

Again, skill refers to the tools and training to do the job correctly and efficiently. These are taught, trained, and developed. Will is the inherent desire to show up, put in the work, and overcome challenges. Learning to recognize, diagnose, and coach to either of these needs to become second nature. No sales manager will ever be successful if they cannot navigate this. So how do you coach to these? Carrot and stick.

The carrot represents rewards, the stick symbolizes punishment. A skilled manager must know when to implement which, and to what degree. There is also the idea of "hitting them with a carrot," but that is much more challenging. As a sales leader, you will need to understand how the individual responds to correction and reward. Many salespeople cannot stand the idea of being praised in front of their peers, others want only that. Some thrive on the fact that they tiptoe along the line of getting reprimanded and the threat of disciplinary actions or PIPs is the juice they need. Some literally wither at the thought of their manager having anything but a compliment for them. This is part of the art form of managing salespeople.

Many people look at those in sales and think, "they're just a bunch of prima donnas." In fact, they may not be far off. However, the good sales leaders can not only connect with their people on the level that they need, but they know how to bring out the very best of them each and every day. I'd go so far as to say that a truly skilled sales leader has mastered the ability to put aside their internal and unconscious bias in pursuit of being at the top. We'll dig into the sales manager persona shortly, but one thing is quite clear. Not everyone can do the job. In fact, I would wager that the portion of the population that can accomplish this feat is far smaller than one may think. I would say that only 2-5% of sales leaders possess the skills and the traits needed to excel at their profession. One thing is quite clear, this isn't a role in which you can force things to happen. Finesse, not force.

The Sales Leader

True strong sales leaders are a rare breed. They are forged from the fires of failure, carved from the mountains of adversity, and sharpened with the dual edge of time and experience. Think that is too much praise? Go do the job for a few years and come find me. I promise you that after your stint as therapist, psychiatrist, financial guru, strategist, and many days as a parent, you'll have a very different perspective on the profession.

Sales leaders who want to lead high performing teams must be Jack (or Jill) of all trades. You wear no less than 5 hats per day, and the only two things you'll ever be short on is time and appreciation. You will put in hours at night trying to come up with and develop contests and games to pull your team closer. You'll know more about the medical issues and relationship problems of your team than you ever, ever wanted to know. You will most likely be publicly praised and ridiculed, your ability to put together a PowerPoint presentation will be something that infects and intrudes on your dreams at night. Your peers will love you one day and not speak to you the next. You'll spend your own money baking cookies and making food for potlucks. You've probably plunged a few toilets and got lost trying to pick up an executive at the airport. You've been in more hotel rooms and missed more flights in a given year than most people will in a lifetime. Sounds really glamorous, doesn't it?

To me and those who call this their career, it's incredibly comforting to endure the craziness. Especially when you get to go on trips paid for by the company. You know deep down that you paid for them in sweat, tears, and probably a bit of blood, but damnit those trips mean the world. Probably the only thing more satisfying is watching your team start to level up and help each other. And there are those days, when your team expresses their appreciation that it suddenly all becomes worth it. So how does one become a successful sales leader? I promise you one thing, it is not easy. True sales leaders exhibit a laundry list of traits that point to success. Humility, ingenuity, curiosity, focus, discipline, creativity, patience, integrity, and most importantly, the ability to understand the long game. You see, sales leaders often get a bad rap. Sometimes it is justified, but more often than not, they are simply misunderstood.

I remember a long time ago, I was on a fast track to senior leadership. The company I worked for had created this program they called "Rising Stars" and those selected for the accelerated experience were invited to more meetings, including one annual retreat where they had the opportunity to mingle with senior leadership offsite, for a few days at a conference. While at this meeting, I spent time with my boss who was also my mentor. After the second day, he and I walked to the other side of the resort to get coffee in the morning. Taking our time before the first session, he asked me what I thought now that I had an opportunity to see behind the curtain, as it were. I responded with the only words that came up. I looked at him directly and asked, "What if I'm not sure I want this life?"

He stood there in silence for a long moment before telling me that was totally fine. We each needed to choose our own path. Ultimately, I did pursue the next level, but I knew very clearly what I was signing up for. I understood the politics, the infighting, the backstabbing, and the commitment it would take to achieve that level of success. I knew I wouldn't sell my soul the way so many had to get to that level, but I knew it would take everything I had. So, I lowered my head and kept my focus on my people. If you get your people across the finish line each year, you'll have an incredibly successful career. Lose that focus, and depression and frustration will derail you. You have been warned.

Control What You Can

It's not a cliché, no matter what anyone says. Have you ever been in a very stressful situation? The kind where your hands sweat, your back tenses, and you swear the entire universe is waiting until you pee your pants? If you can relate, it's probably because you have done some cool things, or because you've been a sales leader at one point. I have never been so far out of my comfort zone than when I was a sales director, yet totally in my element. I lived for it, and yet it caused sleepless nights and waves of nausea that would make any pregnant woman nod in agreement.

The situations that caused the most stress were usually the most benign on the surface to outsiders. It's funny though, it seems like organizations inherently know what causes you the most anxiety and then throw you headlong into those situations like a bookie trying to collect on a debt. Hate public speaking? Great! Here's the topic you'll be presenting on next week. Dislike being the in the spotlight? Awesome, you're being recognized tomorrow in front of the whole company. Hate laying people off? Perfect, someone somewhere decided that an entire department needs to be eliminated and here's your list for tomorrow. This is the life of a sales leader.

If you can overcome your weaknesses, you will thrive. I hated putting together and delivering presentations to sales teams. So, Mike Z decided that was all I'd do for a few years until I learned how to manage the stress. And I presented over and over again, every month. One day after a team meeting, he pulled me aside and told me how proud he was of me, and how I didn't give up but persevered and had become a strong public speaker. If you ever want to find a way to gain loyalty from an employee, praise them in private the way Mike did. I would've marched straight through the gates of hell for him. I went from getting choked up trying to disseminate information to 25 people to calmly presenting financials to over 100 on a monthly basis. I went from dreading standing at the front of the room to looking forward to rallying the troops.

This is the power of coaching. You find what your people hate to do, and you slowly work on it. As they overcome fear and their own insecurities, they find peace and their true calling. Developing sales leaders is a lot like a potter working with clay. It's messy, and you must start over a lot, while there are very few people who understand the work you've put in. But they love the end result, which is a resilient vessel. It should also be noted that working in sales, and developing a high performing team is one of the most addictive things you will do in your career. I cannot recommend it enough.

If you want to get down to the root of this, I've concluded that there are only 3 things you can control, and they must be followed in the correct order:

1. Make sure you breathe.
2. Respond instead of reacting.
3. Make the best decision with the available information.

Controlling your breathing is the first and most critical part of this process. Often under stress, people stop breathing. Doing so is involuntary, but results in the body taking in less oxygen and an increase in carbon dioxide. This causes a calming sensation to come over you. By consciously breathing through the moment, it means you fill your lungs with oxygen, leaning into the stress. You will also create a pause, meaning you can analyze and attempt to fully understand the scope of the situation. This will allow you to consciously think through the moment, creating an opportunity to respond versus react. Reactions are involuntary and often predictable. If you tap your kneecap, your leg should react to that stimulus. On the contrary, a response would be for you to move you knee or block the hit. The former is a reaction while the latter is a response and puts you in control of the situation. While this is extremely basic and a simple analogy, it is the foundational understanding of how we can control our emotions.

By choosing to acknowledge and control your breathing, and choosing to respond instead of reacting, you set yourself up perfectly for the third bit of control- the choosing to make decisions and act on the totality of the information. This three-step process should be completed constantly. Doing so begins to wire your brain to control the only things that you can. It takes time and practice and must be continuously refined.

I think that it is important to stress the benefit of learning to control that which you can. By consistently applying these tactics, you will ultimately change the chemistry of your mind. This is no different than professionals in high-stress jobs. EMTs, firefighters, police, the list goes on. Those not in similar careers or who have not been trained in controlling their emotions will often look at these individuals as anomalies. However, we were not designed as humans to constantly fly off the handle, nor were we ever supposed to always be the victim of circumstances. In fact, it's quite the opposite. We should always strive to remain in control of our emotions, our responses, and our actions. Practice this daily before, during, and after work. If you slip up and react, or find yourself holding your breath, consciously acknowledge it, and try again. We have to undo and re-wire years of bad habits before we can achieve a higher level of interaction with stressful situations.

Pro tip: The best indicator of a strong leader is their ability to control their emotions. Master these, and you will become unbreakable.

There Will Be Conflict

Regardless of your relationships, you will experience conflict. This is as inevitable as the changing of seasons. Everyone knows that conflict will arise, yet many people allow it to derail plans or damage relationships. It's impossible to pinpoint when this shift in perception occurred, but I have my own theory.

I believe that the ability to not only handle but to expect and embrace conflict stems from an overall lack of planned adversity. What I mean is that people who do not consciously challenge themselves, whether it be physical, mental, or emotional, learn to become conflict adverse. Consider an athlete training. They will plan workouts in a particular discipline in order to build strength, endurance, or flexibility as a mechanism to handle the conflict of competition. A research student or professor will spend hours upon hours digging into subjects, foregoing sleep at times to solve challenges or create an invention. An actor or actress will get so deep into characters that they learn to recreate emotions of another person, real or fictitious, and over time they become adept at taking on more and more complex characters.

With any of these individuals, they put themselves through planned adversity in order to become more skilled in overcoming conflict. In fact, they not only plan it, but embrace and seek out this challenge. They know full well that doing this consistently levels up their skillsets and subsequent conflicts are less stressful. So why do so many people shy away from this approach? The answer is pretty simple- it's not easy. Over time, people tend to become more and more like water and look for the path of least resistance. Why take the stairs when there is an elevator? Why buy pen and paper when you can type? Why exercise when you can take a pill? In virtually every aspect of our lives, ease has overtaken effort. Comfort has won out over growth. If you want to get really dark, consider that we are actually marching toward the extinction of the human race by devolving into weaker and weaker species.

There is a very bright spot though. You have the ability as an independent thinker to change course. That's right, you get the option of choosing your path. You don't need to pull a George Costanza and do the opposite in every situation, but rather, start small. Set you alarm for 30 minutes earlier than you normally would each month until you are getting up before the sunrise. Half of the people reading this will initially push back and say that they are not a morning person. There's a reaction instead of a response. You haven't even attempted this exercise before automatically dismissing it. Once you've made the change to getting up earlier, you'll probably find yourself needing to go to bed earlier. In order for that to work, you will probably need to alter your routine before bed so that you are able to get to sleep easier. This may be swapping out a book for watching television or scrolling social media. Maybe eating lighter foods for dinner and not eating past 7PM. Find out what works for you, and then stick with it.

Small incremental changes to your daily routine that you <u>choose</u> to make will begin to have a compounding effect. If you are sleeping better, your mood throughout the day will most likely improve. You will undoubtedly increase your efficiency at work. People will take note of the positive changes that they see in you. And here is the kicker. Once you've sought out and embraced challenge in your personal life, you will begin to approach conflict differently. Suddenly, you tend to expect it, and the anticipation will either cause you to make decisions that will help work through the conflict, or you may find yourself able to sidestep conflict altogether. Talk about creating an environment for high performers!

One of the best pieces of advice I was ever given is to find ways to create adversity for yourself every day. It doesn't need to be a massive undertaking, but rather small doses of discomfort. Work out, forego the fast food and go to the other side of town for a healthier meal, take a walk around the neighborhood instead of plopping down on the couch. Over time, this will create a fresh mindset, and you will find yourself breaking free from a constrained schedule. You will have more time to focus on the things that you want to, instead of always struggling just to get through the day. It's not magic, it's structure. And there is no better cure for conflict than structure.

Now, when conflict rears its ugly head between members of your team, you can't just tell them that they need to create adversity to learn to handle it. You need to provide the tools to assist and support your team so that they can work through the conflict and not have ill will for each other afterward. It may be a good idea to meet individually with the parties involved, to better understand the root of the problem. This should happen before locking them in a conference room like a cage match. That won't end well. It also is not helpful to simply ignore the situation in hopes that it will resolve itself. These things will not magically go away, and if they do, then you have a completely different issue on your hands. I was told a long time ago that if your people stop bringing issues to you, you have stopped leading them. They need to view you as the leader and as such, capable and willing to help work through conflict in a healthy manner. You're probably wondering how to set up this delicate conversation. It is important to not overthink it but prepare yourself to handle a number of potential outcomes. If you already have a good pulse on how your people are doing, then it's likely that you spend a good deal of time talking casually while picking up on potential issues. You know when there is tension between employees, and since it often stems from something in their personal life, having daily interactions outside of pure business talk is crucial. As the leader you need to be able to think and act ahead of problems before they begin to spiral out of control.

Once you have a better understanding of the individual sides of the situation, it is time to bring everyone together. This is a bit trickier than just sending an invite. It is also a good idea to have another person, namely one of your peers, to sit in. They'll have the benefit of not being in the thick of the conflict, and able to view it more objectively. You yourself need to remain objective. If you get dragged into the conflict alongside the other parties, you've been put into a position where you cannot be objective, and you will be engulfed with tunnel vision. I call this sympathy versus empathy.

We've all unfortunately attended a funeral. In doing so, you express your condolences and sympathies. Sympathy means you're right in the middle of the emotional turmoil just like others. But when you read about a complete stranger passing, you are most likely empathetic. You understand what those grieving are going through, but you yourself are not going through the grief process in this particular case. And so, in working through conflict with your employees, remaining empathetic is crucial, but becoming sympathetic removes you from an objective position.

If you allow yourself to be caught up in the conflict, you lose the moral high ground and the position to be of service. You basically throw a massive can of gasoline on the bonfire. You can imagine what the end result will be. Catastrophic failure. I say catastrophic not to be dramatic, but accurate. How will your team look at you if instead of helping them work through situations you constantly become part of them? Spoiler alert, it's not good. They'll lose respect for you in this area, and it's a slippery slope to losing complete control over your team. Whatever you do, be extremely cognizant of your positioning during conflict resolution. You cannot un-ring the bell.

Could This Have Been An Email?

Meetings about meetings. It's difficult to imagine a greater waste of time than standing meetings without clear next steps. Virtually every organization is inundated with meetings, and the average calendar of leaders is busy enough to make you dizzy. Since a sales leader is responsible for revenue, then a simple litmus test should help you determine which meetings you should attend. Keep in mind that your boss may have a very different opinion, but at least this may be a starting point to open a dialogue.

Does the meeting that you have been asked to attend help drive revenue? If you cannot clearly draw a line from meeting to cash, it probably isn't the best use of your time. I had a very close peer who would always remind me that if it doesn't make dollars, it doesn't make sense (cents). I was normally the closet emotional responder in her office, but she would remind me of this adage just as soon as she reminded me to take a deep breath, and maybe a few lunges. If you are confused about the lunges, it's because you can't fly off the handle and do a lunge simultaneously. Skeptical? Give it a try. This mantra will not make you any friends, especially with those in the "strategy" department. Mostly because virtually every one of those teams has never sold a damn thing in their lives, and therefore their opinion isn't worth the time it takes to read their emails. Yes, I said it. I've had a lot of friends who worked on that side of the business, and they just work within a vastly different world. You wouldn't believe the number of times I've had to scream at merchants that I wasn't going to push a particular product because our customers weren't interested in that line at the moment. Lower costs to the company are great, but only if your customers are buying at that time. Case in point, I once got into an actual argument with a buyer who wanted my team to focus on eye protection in December. The only thing that most companies are focused on in December is cold and flu prevention. This was pre-pandemic, but I was in contact with those customers every single day, for many, many Decembers. I knew what they needed and wanted to buy and when. Far too many companies allow their purchasers and God forbid their marketing team to direct the sales teams. If this is happening in your organization, you need to find someone at the top to put on the brakes. Sales directs marketing, not the other way around. Marketing, purchasing, HR, IT, should all be incentivized to prop up and support sales. If it is implemented in reverse, do not be surprised when the company starts laying people off. Those organizations are not listening to the customer. And the sales teams are the direct line to the customer's wishes.

Spending time going through the motions has never built a company or brand. In fact, the seven most expensive words in business are, "That's the way we've always done things." Organizations that can thrive that way can be counted on one hand. And I can guarantee you that they don't make a whole lot of money. Sticking to tradition only works for organizations like historical societies, non-profits, churches, and the like. To be innovative and forward-thinking, you need to break away from tradition and the pomp and circumstance that follow. The good news is that your salespeople will thank you for thinking outside of the box. They crave innovation and working against the grain. It keeps their attention and sparks creativity.

There have been numerous studies on the lack of productivity caused by too many meetings, but I can personally attest to it. At one job, thankfully a brief one, I was running to so many meetings that I literally didn't have time to eat or use the restroom. I'd show up to meetings with the CEO without time to accomplish the laundry lists I had been given every day. Talk about compounding stress. Here are 5 projects I want you to place in priority, and tomorrow I'll give you 7 more. All due on Monday. The lack of common sense and business acumen are rampant in businesses. If I could offer one bit of advice, it would be to raise your concerns in this type of situation. I tried to balance and accomplish it all. I failed. Miserably. Nearly every one of the meetings I was required to go to could have been summarized in an email. And the icing on the cake was that they often scheduled back-to-back meetings in other buildings, forcing me to run between offices in town. Had I not been in the mental state I was in at the time, I would have laughed in their faces and turned down the job. The strategy seemed to be complete chaos. The only two words that came to mind when I was caught up in a RIF was, "thank God."

The Next Chapter

As you undoubtedly already have figured out, being a high performing sales leader is not easy, and it certainly isn't for everyone. I've been asked when the right time is to move on to the next role. As touched on earlier in this book, there are many times when a sales leader must take a long hard look in the mirror. Personally, it is something I do daily. Whether it is preparing for a difficult conversation, an important presentation, or rolling out a new strategy, introspection is key.

The makeup of your team will change over time. Sometimes you'll have a lot of tenured, strong sellers. Other times you'll have a team that you can't even take to happy hour because they aren't old enough. Using an actual mirror, you can refine your delivery or anticipate pushback or questions. You will also come across as much more genuine if you watch your facial expressions as you deliver the messages. You'll be able to catch yourself if you inappropriately smile at the wrong time or appear far too grave when you should be excited.

I'm not sure I know of a salesperson who hasn't employed this technique, and most sales leaders I have worked with also rely on it. The mirror talks, combined with a spouse or close friend to practice with, can be the difference between winning and losing.

Conclusion

Writing this book has been a sincere labor of love. It has brought back so many memories, both good and bad. I've recalled situations that had been buried for years. I'd have to say it has been cathartic and has reinvigorated my career.

Experiences have a way of backing up in our subconscious and clogging our perspective. Getting them out and onto paper breaks up the logjam of creativity and influence.

I'm quite certain that some people will read this and get upset because they see themselves as one of the challenges I discuss. This book is unapologetically blunt. If anything, I wish I had been more vocal in the early stages of my career. I was usually the last to speak in meetings, as I took in the full scope of the issues. However, I'm sure I was passed over more than once because people didn't know where I stood on the matter.

While I have often said that I love animals far more than people, I do have a heart for humans. More specifically, I am drawn to those who are willing to apply themselves to a difficult task, those who without hesitation volunteer to take on such a dynamic, underappreciated career. I love the underdog, the come from behind kind of winner, that can't help but give every day their best effort. It is for those, the ones who emphatically and genuinely help their teams push the boulder uphill that this book is written. For you, and those who have gone before you, I will raise a glass. You are the fuel, the passion, and the drive for thousands of salespeople.

"The happiness of a man in this life does not consist in the absence but in the mastery of his passions." – Alfred Lord Tennyson

About The Author

After nearly 20 years spent screwing up, winning and losing deals, creating some of the best and worst strategies, Joe decided it was time to write a book. He found that most of his good ideas were discovered not in the boardroom, but out running trails and passing miles on his bike. He's been part of corporate America, where he cut his teeth, as well as small tight-knit companies, and found they all have the same thing in common-they are run by people. By being someone who can connect and partner with key individuals, Joe has cracked the code of becoming the liger of sales leadership. From years of leading over 100 employees, to mismanaging one, Joe has discovered a love of writing that he hopes will allow others to avoid the minefields of business.

When he is not trying to convince people to produce more revenue, he is usually found somewhere outside or hanging out with his cats. Joe currently lives in Central Pennsylvania with his wife, working in the Real Estate industry.

Notes

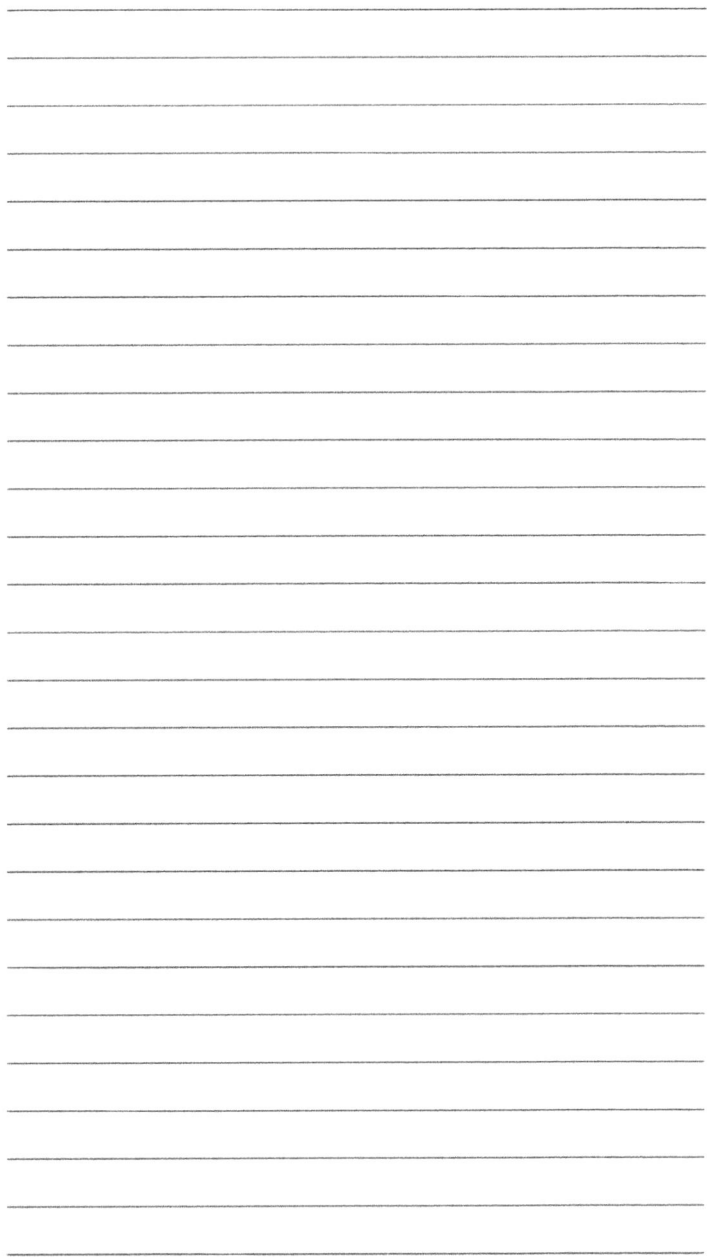

www.ingramcontent.com/pod-product-compliance
Lightning Source LLC
Chambersburg PA
CBHW070123030426
42335CB00016B/2253